Thrum

Thrum

Leef Evans

Turnstone Press

Turnstone Press
607-100 Arthur Street
Winnipeg, Manitoba
Canada R3B 1H3

Turnstone Press gratefully acknowledges the assistance of
the Canada Council and the Manitoba Arts Council.

Cover art: Leef Evans

Design: Manuela Dias

This book was printed and bound in Canada by
Friesens for Turnstone Press.

Canadian Cataloguing in Publication Data

Leef, Evans, 1972–

Thrum

Poems.
ISBN 0-88801-191-1

I. Title.

PS8559.V25T4 1995   C811'.54   C95-920179-3
PR9199.3.E82T4 1995

To Laura, who stopped me from falling

Georgina, who stopped me from spinning

Peter and Sally, for everything else

"Music is feeling, then, not sound."
　　　　　　　　　—Wallace Stevens

Contents

On Sunny Days I Sing to Icarus . . .

Mommy curled me early
in her formaldehyde belly.
Sips & Sips & Sips of iron rye
& scalding sulphur baths, too,
to bring it off.
But I stuck.
Resolute zygote me,
I stuck like snot to the oven door.

Born.

Introduced through the labial curtain
onto the mad stage, me,
a deformed heir to Royalty,
with horns,
a snout wet & wide & black,
ungulate calcial hands;
Bull-necked mute –
a meatloaf tongue to fill my cudding yap –

Born.

Son of Pasiphae.
Minos-child.

1

Born weed-Minotaur,
unbidden. Furled
in the Daedalian maze,
I subsist on sour sapien stuff.
My cud is of blood &
marrow of man fated to absurd death.
& so I tell you,
"Man is rotten.
Woman, too."
There is a madness in Man's meat.
Like quick-silver, it bundles in the gall
& the nape of grey,
coiled like a sleeping asp –
an accumulative toxic boil.

All born
sour, thus,
under the clock's auspices.
Even the best.
But the children
are taffy;
bones like sticks
of cinnamon; spicy-sweet;
flesh like caramel;
soft, fatty &
they break apart
like poached sole.

To my Diet I rage, then,
"My palate is sage, then."
Oxygen-pituitary-time
is the brackish, ochre
gout in the pestilent flesh
of Woman & Man, grown.
Age soils the mind &
drops its septic silt,
unfiltered, into the
tangerine body & makes
limes of us all.
Mommy, I tell you this
through this spittled maw,
"It is kindness, high,
to kill your children
when they are born."

Vessels of Bone

You, he hung Sandbag in the sky;
a gallows' balance
between feather and sun.

Me, he knitted into the Fab earth; coal
for a kiln of crazing pottery;
an obtuse terracotta twist.

On sunny days I sing to Icarus.
Daddy duped us both.

Of Theseus

"All heroes are mad." was
what I thought as
I saw him mirrored, small,
in the sanguine paradise
of plasma running
from my ticked ear.

"Come creature come.
I'll make a vessel
of your bones" was
what the boy said
when he, finally, cleaved
my low skull.

Between Kisses

he told her between kisses
the world's a crystal bauble
that hangs
from the lief feet
of parakeets
& operates
in an existence of sanguine swing
beneath flurious green wings
& jaded, fading things.
Resounding
in this Nonsense Song—
a Nothing arpeggio
in resplendent, captive space.

& if she sighed
it was lost in this Morning's hiss.

The Nymph's Whispers

The world's a generated space
between Monday and Tuesday;
a dull ohming of
change and chance and fancy.
It's an equation of grunts:
the length of my bones
by the konstant of my flesh. Chew
on that, pig.

Beneath her blanket she
whispered this mantra
while he pissed.

Of Marie

Chub chub-a-nub she hummed
between the circus of her meals.
She had long ago become saturate
in her nonsense, finding
one maladroit dawn
an order to her arbitrary spasms.

     Menhir-dad: more salt-lick
     than sapien and his salty wife,
     a pygmied thing so twisted
     in a phantasm of heritage she
     could not breathe without crying
     at a damaged world.

A reservoir of Quirk
the only pocket left to nestle in.
She nestled.
Chub chub-a-nub.

The Eggs of Geese

My father's sister paints on
the eggs of geese.
She paints with whispers
and the soft skin
in the crook of her arms.
She paints Christ in New Orleans
with a gin fizz
and a red velvet whore.
She paints the crotch of a jaguar
roiling through our moist
leafy integrity.
My father's sister paints thin splendid idiocy
on calcium; she paints
yellow yellow things that touch your yellow ear
when the sun sets in September
over the Eastern townships
where her brother's daughter studies Italian
arias and her brother's son
ponders his prodigal hips.
She paints the hub of the Zodiac—
the chaotic cyclic eye; the mad iris;
maniac pupil
round round round the head,
like a tree, ringed, she strokes the
gelatinous mind
for her thin shell circle of friends.
Her Concert flows about the ovum.
And when her heaven's full
we must be content
to dance with late angels
on the eggs of geese.

MOWP MOWP

Take me away baby
Put me in your fishbowl
Make me your love-guppy
We'll eat our young together

Mowp Mowp

Roll
ing off   into
the e   clipse
pillow,   breathe
my opi   um hair (diaboli
cal hai   r   folli   cle). I
fell   I   dreamed.   I saw
you nu   de in my   dreams,
like i   ce cream;   like he
aven; I   ike pla   ted wat   er and
I knew   you were   dangero   us, like
pollen;   like mor   phin ;   like dead
calm. My   fingers   came to   live and
I came   to   feel   the con   centric,
soft pr   int of   my palm;   every rid
ge   I   came to   feel; e   very line.
And when I touched   ed you   I came to
feel your childhood   spread o   ut under
my hand, running   into my pa   lm and con
gealing like pectin; like a glove   of quince
preserved like grandma's cellar;   sticky and
cool on the skin. I came to smell the so
und of your surly hair turning colour in
the summer sun as you ran in the wide fi
ield of your eighth July; your ninth Augu
st.   And I could taste your smile as y
ou cried. Jammed in my hand, you were.
Stolen from the big brown ceramic jar o
n the wide red tile countertop.   You we
e thick and good stuff, before "sticky"
as something I did not like; before t
e religion of bathing;   before I reek
d of puberty; when things stuck to me
nd I smiled; when the great earth co
ected on my skin . . . and I stole hone
y from bees like a boy bear, nimbly
mobiley bouncing in the wind which sure   ly sucked on
me as I did my smarting fist; stuck with honey and stingers of
brave bees. You are under my hand still. But I am awake.
I have no bees beneath my palm now, just spiders. Spiders e
at bees. And though your skin is still smooth
and you are beautiful, the spider in
my palm has left silk by your
eyes and mouth to catch
the hive of your
awake face.

11

a simple chant done in crayon and
smeared with vinegar into the liberal heart

There is no safety in this stuttering love.
I have measured my anger hard (dense),
save for the last part;
soft and ill-calculated.
Not trigonometric or algebraic,
corrugated or fluted,
but fabric-silk and gossamer;
made of lamb's skin and just as insidious.
Whew.

>You screwed the heart out of me
>folded it within your lampas
>and took it to the north side,
>the cold side
>and froze it
>and rubbed it against my belly
>whenever we rubbed again
>and asked would I
>like some of it back.
>I said "yes,"
>but cried.
>It was so cold. And you smiled
>and bit it
>and ate it cold because
>that's the best way to eat that sort of thing.

Soft Languid Hands

Like new soot and tumid air
harboured in the intestines
of a barn swallow,
freckled with shadows of snow
boned with a Conquistador's
teeth ground round and ripped
from the churlish gizzard
of an Okeefenokee alligato . . .

And the especial skin
in the compass of her knuckles
was soft and white
as chewed cotton.

      Hands as soft
      all involve halos
      of insinuate violence.

Counting Waves in Tofino

The sun is the harbinger of
candy and citrus and gum,
but the moon brings
meat.
Carnal butcher. An Engine
of sevens. A Rumbling Oval Prime,
run oblique
into the concentric solar pistons
to mar the mantle
of even mornings;
to machine the sea.

David and I sprawled
on the gneiss
in the honey day
counting waves,
Naked,
feeling the 21st
and 35th mist our
feet and shins and thighs
with salt from the larder.

Habits of Bees

One August eve
she glimpsed
in the apiary serenade
between comb and sea
the coil
of An's greyed brain
in the habits of bees.

This was
a note of sentience
too peculiar to her;
of huge blue water
calm as the lobe
of an ear, hiding
a cosmos
rich as paisleyed yeast.

All that sameness
wave by wave by wave
she could not embrace.
Overwhelmed, she assuaged
her gorged eyes
with old linear harvests.
Damning the madness
of the Span.
Damning the singular bee.

Trash From Heaven

and Jesus creeps in Manitoba's Capital; an apocryphal
smutty plastic sphinx; more crinoline than Christian; more
weave than wool.

and Jesus creeps like cerecloth into the pornographic
pores of every lover's sand and every lover's dream.

and Jesus coils in the small potatoes in my
September-head (oo smooth as the spade in the moist
boiling loam) with chestnut intentions and small dead
birds masticated by a Winnipeg breeze that is mostly
mute; that dries the swallows and drives the litter up the
canyon streets (a polar, amorphous spade turning the
dirt-world fallow-over every every winter).

and Jesus creeps beneath my teeth and swells and swells
and swells; a spit, grown fat and rancid, flushes my vat; a
carnivorous visceral heave that feasts on the pudding of
my Maldoror cor.

and Jesus screams like spastic asphalt that I, I am a child
and more than flesh and bone and cruel syrups; more
than seminal juice; more than trash from heaven.

Rocking Horse Strut

and Jesus slips, a baroque, protozoan slug, into the dark
coop of my cerebellum and tickles it to fits of palsy and
fists of prozac, caressing my queer hair and pulling,
pulling my prosaic tongue thru my groove nose in deuced
dogmatic affection, saying, "God loves you prone, lad; a
Socratic honey-tongued Ionic agapé." Hah.

and Jesus creeps down my nose hound-licking my snot; a
clematis braille down the rail vertebrae to my cyclops and
staff and, with Canaan-Moses-Glory, parts my red sea and
smells the brine of my crotch, dog-hot for clues to my
redemption (done with my cerebral clot, Jesus clatters
where it matters and plucks my balls for guilty weeds).

and Jesus creeps in pantomime, an ocelot-predator-jive,
nude through the grey jungle dawn (Dance you monster
to the nuance of my soft soft song).

and Jesus mines the hive of my spine and locks his teeth
into the short hairs at each end and bends me like a
rocking-horse strut.

and Jesus trills in landfills and empty palms and the quiet
roar beneath the bridge. And he hums the hollow hum of
the deadman's mouth, fern-curled and lolling over the
wheel; the intangible battery between the anode sky and
the humming rod of a man's skin.

Chewed Nasturtiums

and Jesus mewls in the vestibules with Salomé round the
ferrous stain where Jack's brains spilled out; where she
chews nasturtiums, the peppery petals, tumescent blood
on her pointed tongue; where she clucks in his slab ear,
"Grr. The silver dish is a neat conceit for any man's
horizon. Don'tcha think, Tiger?"

and Jesus holds with the caramel Mom—Hard frosting on
my cupcake (powdered and wreathed in baby's breath,
she ate the pomegranate, whole, and undulates lewd with
Pluto in Medicine Hat, now, I am told; gutted pietà; brutal
statuary).

and Jesus, he creeps in all da da Vinci's titterin' virgins.

and Jesus – me, we clambers blue icicles with hands of
wax for Father's waning favour; the petulant heap of
patrician humus. And Dad says, "On, on, on son of mine.
Hang on the rood 'til your skin, shins and sinew turn to
willow, ivy and Morning's Glory; 'til the sweet feel of cool
detritus curls over your fertile knees and you cry to the
vacuum of sophistry; the dried hollow squash." And Dad
says, "Fill that gourd with whatever clay or sagacious
crap's at hand, boy, and swing it, a censer, beneath your
faithless balls and chant to your manifest-cannibal Dad,
heavy on your chain, 'Kumbaya my Lord.' " That's what
Dad says. Nighty-night. Time to cry as orphans cry.

Thrum

and Jesus creeps beneath my Theban sheets.

and Jesus coos into my sonic vegetable an
aural-panic-ballet tucked within your note-note name.

and Jesus, he culls the bile from my bleeding spleen with
pronouns and piano-wire and the whites of eggs.

and he seeps into a second with you—tic-toc-lost but all
recalled. And what is heaven but the stiff morphine-nod
when hell is Memory and Memory's soft awful halls.

and Jesus creeps up the thread over your injured bladder.
The thrum of anaesthetic still curls over you; an ether
memory of a new violence done to you by the world.
Sweetheart, I never meant to be part of your scars.

and Jesus crawls into Thursday to dance with
Wednesday's angel who plucks the wax from my ears—
Sing Sing Sing distant Carolina seraphim—Hang my
anger on your siren peg and dash me to stone; dash me to
stone; throw me to stone; a broken rose on the stone.

and Jesus strums, on his muscle-harp, hymns of crude
salvation.

A Neat Conceit

It snowed today.
It did not snow white so white
it was blue.
It did not snow
trills from fractious clavichords
cascading milky flanks
of suspicious angels.
The snow did not land smooth
as the tongues of glass panthers
(though in a way it did).
It did not overwhelm
the root of sky
like a hoary beard from
some dogged antique god,
unleashed in the
frozen riot of a modern air.

But it did block the sky
somewhat
in rough thin parcels
and there was some small
riot
in the small architecture
construct in my
Brown-not-brown hair
lingering like a ghetto
in my beard
hanging on the banlieu
of my head
making me old.
Allow me this.

This Moon Saw Fit to Touch you in your Casuist Hair and Give you Badgers for a Spine

I I love the soft mammals
that run through your shoulders,
separate your buttocks and bite any stiff Sisyphal dachshund
that might burrow
into your lunar estuary.

I love that like I love
the soft blue Mud Flats of Port Moody.

I like that way you talked
in January
on Oedipus Street
in the fat end of Kokwitlam
in my Phantom-blue Chevy Blazer;
that way you matriculated your porcelain ass
—blitzkrieg across the vinyl seat—
and rolled onto my lap
and ripped the string from my throat
and bent my Pez-head back
and spoke into my weary colon;
that way you reached in and stole my knees
for tambourines and then left
like Salomé with my Jack-baptist-castanet skull
in your smaller-than-cream fist
(a milk bowl for the jasmine cat
that ate the orchids from your father's grave).

I like that way the way I like
a slow, thin cogent edge.

I remember he said, "Damn the grey earth
and the molten petals that curl churlish,
psychotic from the cumulative decay"
Diseased, it seemed,
like that man in Platsburg
that saturday night
that laughed at Janet Leigh
flat in the bathtub . . . last August . . .
it was so hot,
like Jesus it was hot
(I might have laughed myself).

I remember that like I remember
the frozen black mandarins on the veranda on Boxing day.

> We bumped like We groaned & We groaned like a
> bookshelf: in volumes, in stories, in bound pulp &
> paper & particle-board. We were more rutted
> than grooved; more nailed than screwed
> and We broke up as We grunted
> under masticate scholarly weights
> and India India Ink.

> We fucked like that; stuttering; at right angles;
> perpendicular; filling holes; caulking space.

I recall the habitat aftermath,
James Cotton at the "Commodore,"
the Gemini philodendrons tucked in the "Eaton's" hat box,
snow, snow, snow
and quiet.

I recall quiet in that placental month;
quiet like the sound of pulled stitches;
quiet like ice.

♦ ♦ ♦

& You were beautiful then like burlap and eggshells;
like bending pig-iron;
like jaundice.
You were white as Christ's inner thigh.
You were hot like
the point of a pin in the flesh of the ear You were hot.
You were round and vicious like butter on the bare red
element.

& I loved you more than sand
and the soft hum of bank lights
and the chloral madness that roils
between my stick and eyes
and burns a hole through my navel,
corpulent, illiterate and rude.

& I loved You more than that.
I loved You more than that.
more than that.

Everything
Bends

She said light bends.
It bends. Through
the slalom of Black Vacuum, round
the hearts of Stars & Pulsars it bends.
& he said through
an Atlantic cable crackling from
Victoria to Soho; through
a half-second shift
& a dull pause between
sentences he said
everything bends
everything bends
please come home.

Nineteen Twisting Hours in Terminal Tsawwasswen

Smiles like liver and dust
and liver more still, and dust.
Still; not used. Just still.
Still stops (bus stops), still
like liver.
          Talking is not
(or knot) or naught, for nothing
is said, is talked, is smiled.
Not naught. Not nothing. No smiles,
with wheels. Like wheels, around,
the walk (talk-talk), eat smiles
like water; sea water. What water?
No water. Just salt (like tears)
with talk. Just feet, just knees,
just rest. Just standing on blocks;
Cement. Like talk. Cement.
Like liver on wet cement.
With water? Sea water. Like salt.
Just talk with water like tears,
like liver, like smiles; just talk.

I-run-home-
Darling-
Will-you-love-me-if-I-just-walk

I've missed the 11:40
to Nanaimo.
I'll sleep in Courtney terminal tonight.
I'll be kinetic
tomorrow.
So, here's a little of a love
from the day before.

I-run-home-
darling-
will-you-love-me-if-I-just-walk.

Hugs & Kisses

Enough, enough.
I embrace and squeeze
the cruel brass staff
that is my moral equilibrium.
I am nothing
but piled meat and sharp teeth
and bad manners.
I am composite waste of funnel fate.
I assume
you emulate.

I bubble into midnight
and ignore the vert to chat with asphalt.

I bubble into ash
and spit at Sol
hiding in the city's umbral laundry.

Cached in the street, spawned here, I waddle
the walk with Crown Royal cranked through my
vault soul and sing to you, Mater and Pater,
that I am your exhaust and diffuse in a
monoxide puff
behind the manifold of your joining;
that I am comprehensive, malgamate legacy.
I am you (only thinner
and thinner) and will die after you die
—Solomon miseris socios habuisse doloris—
eh?

I am diagram
        constructed moody
print from the unconscious dogma of
unconscious violence.

I am precious precious
refuse;
a rip-snortin' boy boy
Cain in Nod. Harpy-hatched,
I am coo coo and bundle and crowd out
my pin-feathered brothers from
my pin-feathered tenement
and nurse on unlikely nipples.
I am evil? So be it, daddy.
I am yours.
Kiss kiss.

Mom

Mom was made of sponge and small noises. She thrummed through the framework of our cottage like leaves. She was handsome as the devil himself and as transient; made of cream nylon, new lettuce and tumid air; fraught with coiled rope and the faint odour of Edam. She was a structure of amorphous stuff. Sometimes nearly nothing but skin and vinegar; the next moment bombast-solid like ham. She was furtive as steam. She could round a corner like midnight's new minute. She was there, where before was only a neutered space in a chafed architecture.

She was cantaloupes and accordions, rash violet mornings and baked hovis bread. Her face ate up a room. Her body was a genius. When she left at six I wept for a week. She must, I thought, have left to play the cello with Orpheus, or to mine the moon for diamonds, sing folk songs to angels in the Grand Canyon, or have left for Afric shores to caress the spots off every leopard and send them in a sealed jelly jar to the Pope, for Christmas. I never believed she left me to serve mud and eggs to Regina's rectal dirt-workers; to shack up with a vagrant pipe-fitter; to have other children. I never believed this. I don't believe it now.

Now I know no more of her than the remembered brilliance of her treacle body; her spasm-form. It coalesced and cooked a room into custard shape. She was quince to my little simpering jammy life. And she left me shredded and hung with her hurricane husband. She left me. She left me. She gave me the soft nipple to my soft palate. She gave me her coagulant smile. She gave me mass. She gave me a pernicious balance and then she left me bleating in the sweet early autumn; december looming. It is not that she took, but she took what she gave. Better to have suckled me on thistles and wasps and to have clotheslined me out in November's long storms. I am haunted by Persephone's six seeds. I am blanched by the ague of a fatted young heart. Better my chest be made lean from birth and so comprehend fasting-bastard-life, than chew on this comb of honey. Be weaned on the cleaved plain with nothing but a pell, skinny man to give flat care to my scaggy, Maternal-brown, Cold Turkey Shakes.

Even now, I am crocheted around her four corners. Even now I am hiccup.

Motor
Clay

everything builds down
relentless;
a need to be
round and circle dirt.

The finite clod.
A centrifugal eclectic paste or
senate of brown or magnet of colour or
reservoir of horde;

Yorick and Yorick and Yorick.
The only democracy is death. Clay.
The skull of earth in which
all sink and fuse and grow and moil.

Cyclopaedian Butter-Man Song

Butterman pulled his sophist pud
too long
and has gone blind as
a cashew.

"Tell me" I recall
he asked the last
Autumnal equinox when pumpkins
were green as peas and Saturn
spun into the naked sky
and made rude noises – the farts
of digested children
(it was that kind of Fall).

"Tell me. Where
have you hidden my lungs?
The air's so thin
and I need 'em, you see,
to feed my naughty skull
which is, even now, licking
the dew from my cerebellum;
hungry for the raw oxygen gruel. Where
have you . . . my
lungs? You took 'em
last thursday
to carry vegetables from market
and I never
got 'em back."

He was seeming mad.
I told him so.
I said "Fool"
winking to my friend.
"Recall. You sold
your bags of breath
to the young Bishop of bric-a-brac
on Bradley Lane,
to buy laudanum
to soak your o'er-dazzled eyes.
Hush. You've
forsaken inhalation,
the pawn of luxury,
for an affixed and sundry seeing."

And he raled
in the corner, weeping,
while Liverpool evened
at Anfield.
This is what comes from too many
Faustian fugues and
too little of Helen's Chimera-Melody.
We told him so
as we drank our stout
singing
"oogie oogie oy oy."
"You'll never walk alone."

Serpent, African, Animal

Snake will swallow
its own tail and
will not go hungry but
its Universe is compromised
by its spine.

Like the Algerian
who eats existential gelatin
in the vacuum of his dresser;
Albert, who starves on a largesse
that distends his belly
with wax apples
and unethereal cereals
and sweet breads from Circe's howling mill.

But a Beast eats
circadian venison
and emetic lunar grasses,
Grunts in massive fashion,
heavy as Grendel,
more solid than Sootka spruce.

A Corpulent Okanagan Gentleman

Felton Hammer sold pears to tourists
in Kelowna and spent his winters
in Vegas consorting with chafed women
and chafed men, singing "I sell pears
in Kelowna to you and you and you," smiling
over his continental breakfasts, dreaming
of the demure and felt green
and the calcite orbs that represent creation, numbered
like ordered cherubs.

In Excess, Continual,
There is Cure of Sorrows.

More of Me's in my
shadow's abstract crawl
than in gruelling dissections
of my silly cell.

Don't mark me by
the gyre of my corpse or
my derma-flair stasis.
Fast past this frame I go go
so you should note me
in the scent of my
wake and the yaw in this metamorphic ship's
isostasy-tipple, as
I gnaw on Gaia's gritty tit,
in reeling, chaotic orbit.

More angel than idol
and I've wings, if only
in an atmosphere
of Being; feather-rattling
in the air of this
rolling meat-clock.

Absurd Denim

I have, on my pants' legs,
painted St. Christopher
with child,
and painted, also, a platypus
ballooned from a
dictionary cartoon.

If these things are
not alike
they are like now,
scintillant in
the cinema of my
strobal gait.

Here, St. Cristopher shimmers
quiet
with angelic marsupial,
while a criminal boy
with webbed toes, haloed
nose and barbed heel ponders
the enigma of his stitch.

Carbonaceous Mewl

I told her that no creaky
deus ex machina
will reside in her blossom palm or
in her silk palate; that
language will not flit
about around her like
a gadfly and pick
at her stray ribbons.

I told her the tremors
she felt were only me
swallowing
in the brusque megaphone
of the burlesque
January air,
cold as hell and
resonant as a gong
(where I resurrect her
every dawn
in brass cataracts –
a gold litter from a blood's
lush roil, I told her).

What I told her
she did not hear,
pulling these cambric sheets
off her brutal shoulders
and breathing in,
like a beast,
the flesh of the air.

Hot Plums'
Umber Hum

Jacob's small hands
are harps.
Raucous twiddlers
of manifold passions.
Twang.

Jacob's wee hands
are harlequins
of inky nail and knuckle
that harpsichord cross
his sweet's half-acre;

l'il fingered naves
that pick and trill
an abdominal score
in the banjo groin
of Guenevere's high
vaulted crotch.

Footnote: in the journals
            of concubines
            it is the jazz of fools,
            not a King's concerto,
            that cracks the ragtime polyp.

Messiah

I lay down on my Beefeater Posturepedic
on the west bank levee
of the Pitt River
at midnight
in June,
seven Januaries since the first hair on my balls,
three days before solstice
singing "Stewball was a race-horse"
to the crickets and stars,
marvelling at how the earth adhered to my spine,
sensing the centrifugal surge
in the fluid in my eyes and the vitriol in my gut,
telling the Lord of all this nonsense
he could go home
as I was the isoscelent leg to creation.

Zool Wooed by His Lover

"There is" he muttered
"a navigate to any day
and when the sun goes down
there is not nothing
in no one but
a gibberish hope it will
rock round and rise to what,
by habit, we call the dawn."

The other said to him "This is
the spit of an avuncular
pedant; a threadbare knit
of greasy chat.
It's enough, I think,
to have your balls hang long
in August's umber hum and
eat hot plums at four
to know an orbit is involved."

This lewd empirical won him.
Epiphany for Polyphemus and, in it,
he grinned yellow as a yolk.
"Evening, then" he spoke
"is the sound between the sun?"
"And the cello moon
is the periphery of an ear." Excited,
the other added
with a flit and a flourish
and a capricious hind.

Prometheus' Spawn in Grease Paint

A young boy
might sit and watch the
dusky dusk
dusky-up and watch the
distant highway traffic
headlight-up his room
with mottled nightmares;
dancing shadows from
a far off apple tree;
branch over branch
over branch over branch.

He might look on
the clown on blue
velvet hanging on
the blue wall;
looking at it an-
imate in kaleidoscope-
silhouette-horrorshow,
twisting with all the prickly
Gothic nausea of
née Wollstonecraft's corporation
of meat and sutures.

The clown might
utter sweet things then,
when language and umbra
become rude paramours
and enounce from each other's
lesioned backs. It
might,
in its Vargas-Karloff leer,
hand him a
bouquet of brooding
gentians (chalked with
napped madness) and say softly
"Sorry your cat died, boy." Clown
lips large as eggs, eyes
like pools of hepatic fluids.
What boy would not
then believe in
veracious tangible shadows,
branch over branch over branch?

Heritage

No.
He was not clumsy.
That's not it.
There wasn't any
dropped spoons or
spilt sugar in him.
It's just he had
no shadows and seemed
pasted on my eyes
so I couldn't see
around him.

Foolscap-man. He'd
slice your sight, utility-keen.
A graceless sheet of heat
and hairs and hands and feet;
arms at evil angles
warring with his cor;
his legs a millhouse
of hard china and hinges.

It hurt to look on him
like it hurts to rub
and old white scar.

Thomas and Tina
Dreaming of Lima

They danced an Andean jig
on New Year's Eve
in ever-diminished wheels
like a Cyclone
turned on its ear
or an otiose orbit, oh.

He stole into her pink
Peruan hide
and smirked nude smirks –
a conscious flamingo
with thin legs
and upside smiles to glean
the brack
for little bits
of her Titicacan silt.

The Coffee-Roaster Man

There, surely Marie, is a man
you could love.
His locomotive elbow
piston-humps 50 kilo sacks
of strong Kenyan or heavy
Columbian umber Meld.
A left arm, large as
a bobcat, swinging
parcels of black gauche
et guache et gauche encore.

He looks like
the fiddler crab.

Surely, Marie, such asymmetry
must suck the
smile from your simple chest.
Let him viol
the steam of
your roasted beans
and bury your face in
his murky cacao chest
dark as a continent,
a musky emperor of scent.

Leda and the Swan

Zeus was no Swan,
but a goose.
and Leda (but no, not yet).
With feathers domestic, gnat-ridden
and floppy in flight—a loose god—
and Leda (but no, not now).
He did strut and hiss
like any twitchy, haemophiliac king,
Phat with passion, phairly clumsy
with rudder that was anchor and chain
and did ball him down
to an earth that wud take
his ethereal seed and be quite the same
for all his goosey efforts.

Now, Leda fed him fat
on a string
from her men-
strual ring and soon
had all gods, feathered
and flesh, tethered to her
construction. Squawk and flap
as they may, their order
on line. Dumb
fowl line, tail to
beak, beak behind.
A feral Order, strung like easy-beads
to the rhyme of her great vagina.

Though Zeus be Jove be An be God; though
thick hands grip broad biblical soil and grind it
under bollix nails,
still, no thick fist can squeeze real
anything
but duff clay, sand or dust
from the palpitating crust;
Not as the maternal palm can
embrace in its injunctive knuckles, all
that is malleable
and press round-out
from the crescence of its grip
living stuff—
wet, unconscious, humped.

LIGHTNING TURNS
MAN INTO WOMAN

– newspaper poem –

Burly Martin Camacho
that crack in your mantle,
and your congenital turnstile spun.
You felt your penis curl up
like a salted snail
your latin hammer chest
thinned in sinew bone & muscle
and your animus pins rolled.
The spare rib rounding;
mammae bulbs pushed.

Tiresius was, in like,
drummed up; cudgelled
into feminine flesh.
He spent seven such summers
in trans; in
Phalluslessness;
made then myopic,
June-blind, for seeing
the tumescent gap.

But how long for you
Burly Martin,
and what compensation?
How far can you see? when
your wife of thirteen
year and children
twelve ten and seven
cannot see nor believe in
your pumice grizzly mug
gone soft as birth.

or do you care?
In this puzzle-fuck,
have you found something curious;
more than lost manhood?

You work in Fragrances now
at Belk's downtown;
the fabric of your flesh
perhaps pleasing in its bias –
a perverted Lamia, you
coo Obsession with some sweet
youth of Corinth, curling
his listed ear
with your musty tongues,
rich in masculine overbite.

Immersed now in Strange
coy manners that tickle
the upper pockets
of your lathing smooth legs . . .
'til some old sophist lout
should call you out
for the snake you are
and you shrivel
from your youth
and boil into myth
Mrs. and mystery.
Like Lamia,
it is a penny-truth
that makes you mist,
and the pedantic,
suburban thunder
that really rattles
your androgenous skull.

An Animate Architecture

—in my room—

In my room (I have stripped
to paint it). In my room
I have stripped
to sleep
and thrown the derelict's mattress
mid-floor where—
the soft-edged polyhedron –
it lies with lines aslant;
dynamic to Mother Cube
that wombs us both
(soft-bodied forms).

Sitting stripped,
squinting
in bright light, I ta-tap-tap "these,"
these black smacking stamps
its spattering keys,
a staccato melange on this
thin thin thin slab-thing;
an albino square thing
with its Frantic ink heart.

Squatting,
hung from the near naked bulb.
A fingering light source.
Calder would have me
(as I am now; spinning
within) hooked on the bulb's
umbilical strand;
hung.
A spider's meal

tired and mistwisted
i sit on a tuffet
eating my words away.
the room's down beside me
beneath me, astride me.
i'm frenetic, synthetic, awry.

I am old old ant
in ice blue amber.
Roll this box about
and see my flesh
in slow exposé.
My limbs are perfect;
my legs tucked coy
beneath my butt,
hands away
from my bolt by
my ribbon arms.

If you,
as god,
were to section this cube,
would you be bright enough
to see me
in planes,
or would you just see
an egg
with square white
and bloody yolk?

Rebeca Fuseli

In her sack of off-orange crêpe
and nylon she carries
an upper plate of
an older lover – convinced now
it is the upper plate of her
old man; dead in the schism
of oxygen when he drove
his D-9 cat, lurchy, into the
pas pas Pacific off Kitimat;
where his dentures sought
liberty through his open yap,
settled on the goop floor,
and become incorporate in
the carapace of an assassin
crab where he walks the
seas, now, smiling like crazy.

In her sack of peach cloth
and salmon weave she totes
a left shoe from a pair
of magenta pumps (so red
they hum), bought at a
Used Christian Clothing Boutique
(Ms. Magdalene's p'rhaps).
She imagines it's her mother's.
She imagines her mother
wearing it on the
corner of Hollice and Sackville
swinging her overripe, maternal-bent
hips toward every passing
station wagon for the
lachrymal Halifax danes who'd
have more Gertrude than
Ophelia in their horizontal
tragedies.

In her sack of garbled puce chartreuse
she saves the severed,
Raggedy head of a doll
she nicked from Eaton's
last Easter that was so
like the doll her Uncle
tore apart that second
week of April when all
the dogs died
and somebody's blood
piebald the basement
sheet rock.

In her sack of ochre-flesh-textile angst,
with head and shoe and teeth, she wombs
rich velv loam; handfuls
of Fraser Valley silt
she keeps damp damp
with stale pepsi.
Alone,
she might (she might) sink
her hands deep within her sack,
sickly perfumes of old cola
charging her loft
as she rummages through
the sands of Morpheus,
fingering soil
for the fossils of her days,
stroking the fetid red hair,
caressing the rotted grinning face
and its skull of fluff
while dentinal plastic
and a vinyl pump
become castanets in the
muddy syrup,

clicking a flamenco-cicada
serenade that suffers
as an evening lullaby.
Click. Click. Clack.
Like the songs of whales
or the scratching
of a coffin lid.

The story is not so sweetly squeezed from my shrewed skin

A quintessential gravel road
of inherent youth; inherent memory.
Dusky, caulked with imagery.
Walking barefoot,
feet calloused and black on an oiled gravel road,
I saw the yellowing peel
of a dead hopper
on the crest of a small hill
neath the agnostic foot
of an immense Pine
that's long since bent to earth;
as the wood has long since gone rot on Golgotha
and the rose has gone soft to dust.

A dead insect: angel to me.
The son to my young crew-cut mind
(as the little dead are all jesus
to small children
that they may witness god).

In a dust over the carapace
crawled an elbow of hunter wasps,
crooked over, and bent.
Militial. Roaming.
They did not sense me drop
that small apocalyptic
stone on them.
Thud.   It rolled, sentence passed. Thud

a mottled cream of insect flesh,
tangerine and yellow-white,
with the wild jack-eye of christ
whispering wild from the thick blue dust guts
of the martyred locust.

And there was no changed
  perspective; just a
  slackening in the eyes
  and a fever in the ears
  that has never seen
  fit to lessen.

Your Paper Ear

It's that we spit our goodbyes
that I write.

I ask no reply.
I am leaving for a long ever
in a short while.

So I whisper
isolate here
in your paper ear
and let you know, dear, you were wrong
(I did not love you easily
but quickly).

And, if it's not
ridiculous
I love you still,
in a wretched crack,
in a rolling soul that also holds
the folded note
of a flat goodbye.

Once a Man

I was a man in ninety-three
with heavy step and heavy knee
and solid hip and fuller brow.
I was a man in fall, I feel.
My soldered body told me so.

On the knoll
on grass and earth and bones;
kneeling in October's lungs
on a hump of the Millenium's knitting,
Ucluelet's Obelisk, I sit.
Column to song;
puerile song
in the purple air,
Chanted
to blood and charcoal and cool summer mud and crayfish eaten
by ducks and ducks by
raccoons, raccoons by serpent roads.
Sung. Mumbled. Then hummed
and, in humming,
lost to hub caps,
straight razors
and the chit of a linear minute
and I am no more boy no more.

I was a man in ninety-three.
My solid body told me so.

Big Smile

The Big Smile, when the lips turn
up and the saline track is parallel to the
enamel blades.
The Big Smile, when the inner
rib is rent up through the throat,
frayed like a straw and shows
as a grin under aching cheeks.
The big smile is the ice in the hot dry
cheeks after she's left and her
hot body and cold mind's a crêpe memory.

     Oo chucks Oo
     An isometric incisor screw
     into my happy O happy ducts.

The Big Smile coarse simple and mean
and God I am cogged metric
in The Royal Machine: a ground
superior work cast in inferior alloy:
Pretty-Brittle as chicken bone
Hell-Hard as black ice.
Dark as guts that're bound in blood
—blue oozing oxygen—
til the Coeliac grinning slit rips wide rips white rips even
and I smile bright from my button-hole
an umbilical carnation grin.

     and the pain is mine
     I made it
     mugging in the Vincent Price air.

The Big Smile from eyelet to spleen
and   God   potential like everything like everything
you gave me, but you spooled it
round a rotten fool of wood; And I would,
you knew (in your RC JC sense of humour), be
a ball of clever string, knotted with loose ends;
tangled tragic.
No Real Smile, no way
for this cowboy O boy.

      and I've informed my clavicle
      that solitude is a brittle, caustic
      blade that splinters in the flesh,
      and that You are as hot as vinegar in the wound.

The Big Smile   (through sanitary teeth)
the pins run down also
bellowing air from
the mortal furnace
– leave me oxygen,
depraved carbon,   shit
from the shoulders;
my head so far up my ass
it comes full circle.

      ah Darling, pooh.
      When gravity is fucked
      and a countenance that
      should drag on the gravel is bent into my hairline

The Big Smile
that sucks from your hips
and curls round your ears
like a vaudeville beard.
The Big Smile
my skull dripping, melting
from the furnace of my blazing-angel-baby head,
Grim acetylene cutting my
sinus & eyes,
hot enough to boil stone;
dripping white sugar bone
through my soppy gums;
dripping flash-acid
into my temporary soul

And it was your needle glance Love,
cranked in my bicep flow;
it kept me mean;
it kept me even and unclean.
A fine opiate spirit in your eyes
when we met
is now cheap street heroin.
I've jaded nipples in my arm
and you are (still) all laced, and fine
in my baby-carriage mind;
a remainder of my gaunt affection,
where my lips curl up, malnourished
and thin as pounded gold,
to show my incidental, crazy teeth
that hang like earrings from my eyes.

Coelacanth

Shunning god and darwin, both.
Crimson coral-eyed.
Living Shell.
Barb to sleek Extinction's side.

I am, I am the murmuring coelacanth
and I need breathe, always,
the glut of your deep, deep seas.

I was hatched before the lord
in your brood womb
and massive-flew in your blue-uteral space
as you saw fit.

But. Man. Now I'm ripped
like rude sinew
out of your Velvet stuff
and this atmosphere is lacking
and this skinny air hooks all over
my frightened skin,
and my barrel-core is a swollen cause
with pressure well-buried in your viscous oval hole.

I will, I will rupture.
Disgorged and naked, I must explode;
bloated on nitrogen,
bending violent and base.
Deep-sweet, rise.
Vise, then, these scaled, malformed hips
that scream in barbed-wire wind,
and crush in my swollen chest.

I am, I am bleached,
on black sand.
So send a curling emblem,
an umbilical tug,
and lick me off
this Everest hell
with its thin Oxygen
and petty Madagascar anglers.

Roll my phosphorous soul
round-hot back into
your primordial gut.
Give me, again,
that heavy tongue.
Feed me that brine-honey-air
where I will swallow tonnes
to breathe just once.

coelacanth

juggernaut
heaving shot
scaled Atlas; a Universe
of balanced brine
on your dumb fishy spine.

Wraith of permanence
Smeagel-eyed.
Vicious in the limbo
below your ceiling
hung within
the chandelier ballast
of your helium spleen.

Your iron soul
curls in the molten-cold
ocean hold.
Tempered
and anchored to oblivion
a mass of aeons
round as Age
no corners of change
left to you and yours.

Man and Boy

We're not Monks, you stupid flatulent, cocksucking bastard.
We are Man and Boy. We are Male,
atom and joint. We will know one Birth;
just one. Our purpose is in our pants;
a trouser-fulcrum.
Cry if you will, but it's at least easy to see.
Our thing is short and brutal; only a legacy to
tomorrow. Someone other's soft agenda. We've
no menstrual ties to the Gaian ferment. We are
Man and Boy. We roam. We spawn
with the habits of passion. We die. We're blessed
simple things. Drones that pose
and are chosen and thrown out with the comb.
This world views us as Autumn's Gone'
seasonal
fertile humus. We are contractors
to the sky and other liars; subletting niches of creation
for small dais of cedar
and pedestals of maché.
The sublime is a radish and
makes us burp. The colossal's our banquet. We must
overwhelm. We must walk square
and heavy and loud. We must
revel within all that grunts and is rash, petulant, stupid.
Man and Boy know this best.
We are Man and Boy.

Rabble Exodus

The wind resonates in Prince George
like Colonus' Furies;
like the white broadsheet of Hecuba's gaze.
Hey. Let's you and me leave this shredded hell.
Let's turn to Metropolis
and dance with Come-along prostitutes;
sheeted in nickel, cooled in crude;
let's suckle nickel tits, tickle nickel thighs.
Let's be winched, run over or
beaten dead with sensualist clubs.
I don't care.
Let's be somewhere,
elsewhere, other than here
where we sip desperation every morning
from the abandoned dew
on our abandoned lips; where
we call out to a lone dawn
that we are the rugged last bastion
of individualism; that we chew arêtes
and spit moraines; Bunyon-dummies
Let's leave The George, father. Find
a woman and sink your hate into your balls,
soak morning sheets and be done with it. Find
the Phoenix Phuque and curl out of your colic.
Choke out a life. Find
a smile on your morning left, make coffee
and crumpets and sit on the veranda
and talk about her white knees
and bitter histories (others, also,
have cringed in the wind, you know).

Killing Father Off Tofino

Am I a fisher of souls, Daddy?
Daddy, when I did you
calm on the Pacific edge;
when I slit a second cool smile
in your gristly neck;
when I threw your narrow angled body
into the fundamental storm
w/ leaders knit into your ribs
and anchors stitched into your hips;
when you sank Michael-like
into that blue in blue hell;
can I be, am I a fisher of souls?

Hope you're happy Daddy.
Hope teal Dis holds more than this
dirt-dull heaven ever forked over.
Hope the water's rich w/ bawdy witches;
corpulent whores who'll drive iron
into your clouds
w/ their full, rollicking shanks.
Hope they sing ornamental, tasselled canticles
& are ever biting your criminal ears,
licking your lobes and sour eyelids
w/ their sugared spittle and candied tongues.
Hope and hope the dogfish and halibut
are scaly seraphim with cherubic fang
that they tear your madrigal soul over seven tender seas.
A Daddy's soul deserves more space;
more space than the skinny naked berth of doric heaven.

When I cut your pipe and you choked
on the mob of oxygen;
when I sang to the ichor oozing from your neck
& kissed your cheek and lowered you
—a rude pietà—
into that Macbeth-November night,
Duncan's eyes rolled in as yours rolled back
& I cried aloud at the jocular jackpot
in the Kingdom between Father and Boy,
while what's Female in me went crazy
in the oscillate landscape between
cool sheets and a thin blade.

When a father is buried,
a mother is burned
and a boy is baptized
in ashes and loam.
Christened in mud and fossils,
I am wide as rotting flesh,
        vast as methane.
I am married to death.
I am son to the dun pulse of the stopped heart.
I am a fisher of souls.

Inkidu

I measured time with my groin.
Lepoard, Wolf and Bear
walked the rock I walked
with much the bias I walked with; with
the same orbit round Uruk as I.

There is a weird space
between street and field;
between my mean eye teeth
and the molar aggregate.

When I was fucked into avenue
by the osmotic whore
its hard to tell whether
my urbane brother filled my Fang
or honed my grinders before he
refined my horny tail and gave
passport to my hide.

Maudlin in Montana

She stood sentinel on the cusp
of a Razor Montana dawn;
Grey Helena on the piss-yellow horizon wire;
the spine of practical architecture
curling out of the plain
like a hunching dog.

♦ ♦ ♦

Sub-Cumulus,
in a Big Sky cornfield
she sang "I pang
for destitute food
to succour the lice in my heart.
Give me that Melancholy licorice,
Black & Salty & Odd."

The dead ears of Mass
gave nod to her timpani
& swayed
a small, morose degree
to the concert left.
A cold front, creeping in
from the colic plain,
threatening
a passionate wave
of insidious shivers,
told her someone or other's
brother had died
& that the earth was still a quilt
of rash & vicious knits.

God is Horizon; is Periphery; is Transluscence.
God is Diffusion; is Humus; is Wane.
The Thing moves smooth through the mouth of the eye
when its corners are blurred; where image is married into
image is married into image is married into image.

The landscape is Halo; an ecstasy of distance.
Atmosphere is breath of clay; clay is tongue to air.
The mouth is round and makes things round.
The eye is round and makes things round.
Nothing ingested has edges.
Wyoming is Being.

It's assumed the father fell asleep in the early morning on the upgrade into the Black Hills. There were no skid marks. The beige Chrysler Mini Van seemed never to have slowed down. It just veered into the path of the Peterbilt barrelling down the hill in the opposite lane. The semi had locked its brakes for some thirty metres before the impact. The marks were clear and black and thick as tar, and long as a life itself. The driver of the rig tried hard to avoid collision. There was red paint scraped from his machine on the bored stone bank that spoke of this effort. Fated stone that saved him from rolling and doomed the family of three from Madina, Ohio. What must the truck driver have thought as, time slowing, he saw the lolling head of the father snap up finally, too late, as the truck's headlights lit the interior up into a vortex of radiant, flailing light—death imminent as the dawn? Was there time for screams or gasps of fright or surprise? Did the little boy see it all evolve and think this was only the way of driving hills blasted from stone; not recognizing his father's error; having no life-barometer other than a father's seeming omniscience?

Driving by, B. felt the hiss of blood like a siren of surf, loud and crashing cross the tympanic membrane, smoothing footprints in his head; smooth like a mussel's spine; smooth as onyx knives. One mere, red line of blood, like a red ribbon tied to the blow-hole of a metal-flesh balloon, crack-flaccid on the earth like a pillowcase of glass, trickling red in small perverse urges across the cambered road to be flattened and smeared by curious traffic; traffickers in the Great macabre song of Rolling; rolling fifth-estate and centipedal through the Doppler-snap of the scene, giving it place and time (where it hung before in a twisting limbo of Chirico-asphalt; Columned in dusk and dusk's teal Colonnade); giving it lungs and lips and in the eternal drum. B. felt the journalist ghoul hang, boutonniere, over his heart and burrow like a yellow worm into the song of his retinue.

Contemplating Abstract Cats
and Shadows of Mass

An ash Manx walked the mantle ledge.
Its paws whispered above the blaze.

She nudged the globe a bit
and lapped some water from her dish.
There were scraps of paper
on the table,
chairs strewn about the yellowed room.
Sedan and Hack and Truck broiled
on the hot asphalt beyond the glass (a
happenstance of magicked sand).

Those crumpled notes
mobiled his thoughts in pensive jum jum
and those chairs and tables
were molecular anagrams
for the mime-sinew of the streets;
an aping of the drab coil of Earth
and its frantic-shiver-stick: the
chaos of the moon.

The Sphinx's crypta
hissed from the rough feline tongue.

carolina

Raleigh. Tobacco Hub.
(Words that carry on the boiling air
carry to the coast
and loaf like cryptic yokes
on the shoulders of shrimpers.)
Bryden wakes and rolls and registers
with the morning sun
and hums cruel licks (the air jazzes
everything up). Bryden watches
The Kudzu lean forward in the new warmth of dawn
and yawn a green yawn;
an awful emerald beast.
Like a cheezy 50's creature from
Planet X-12 come to leech
B.'s unctuous sins from his unctuous skin
and transport them back
in frozen yogurt form
to its suckling, Triffidy young
so that they can feast
on a Sapiens-compost.   boy.

But mostly there's Tobacco. Tobacco.
Stacked.
Brown leaves,
Spined hides.
An obscene tannery of green.
Small fossils of a southern season
Rendered into litanies of ritual and habit
and dry dun fragrant jam. B. feels it still,
reeling in the land and air
and landing like butter on his burn;
like sour balm on his festering pecan.
                    Weird.

Carolina

Sounds of flesh on flesh
in flesh on sand in sand
in heavy air at
night gave
way to syrupish Myrtle Beach hauntings.
He sang in one long drone
"I recollect her and the oval
her-hammer of the waning moon
boiling white oil off her shoulder
and the scalloped, teasing olive-sheen
of her smiling face-beam as she
drawled dreams
and carved dreams in the pearl air
in front of me,
like drowsy Marzipan animals—
Almondy, lusty and groping.

"Her id-blue eyes like rockets
of salt in the Fourth-of-July shaker of time,
hinted intimations of Hurricanes;
of shifted structures;
moved homes.
And I shuffled
in the sweet almond churl,
and was buried in beige paste
and ivory sediment and cultureless
lunar beauty.
I was Swallowed and Gone."

Bryden spun
on the medallion sand
under the spotlight sun,
and on tiptoes, swore
he could see the distant Pacific;
the cold cold Atlantic digging
the meanwhile-grit beneath his Achilles;
Penelope's perfume
costumed in the pantomime
of years. Sniff. Redolent-
Bitter-Pheromone and Odysseus dead
in the stomach of Troy.

Never Goin' to Mexico

There are borders in my body; places
devoid of moisture,
full of sand and scorpions and skeletons
and the granite of Pocaqatapetal.
The consul died on the day of the dead
when I was twelve.
I have lived too long along these shores
of Deep Cove dreaming of
inebriate deserts lolling under
the dull threat of candy skulls, embalming ash
and Malcolm's pumice-script.

Lady Macbeth in Alabama
(as told to Ophelia in Austin)

Her cloak was red; so red inside
when she sauntered
mad down her stairs,
wiping
a residue of duty off her sublime knuckles,
I admit I fell for her.

Her legs
were the whites of sleeping eyes.
They unsheathed,
with every stride,
from the satin foreskin of her shift
reminding me
of queer nightmares
and the soft space between
closed eye and oxygen.

In audience
I became Thane of Masturbation,
bedding the insane heroines of Avon, kissing
their aortae, nibbling
the shadows of their blood.
  Did I mention her cloak
  was blood red in
  its tremulous folds; neither
  menstrual nor chaste-rent?
              I think I did.

ORANGE IS BLUE
LIGHT IS BLACK

[Always that danger of immersing yourself in the manners
of others and losing the momentum of your own birth]

Eating fruit in the scintillant
blue; the figment-lamp
in the privy on the Greyhound, mumming
the moon over the Smokies
when we were lying together
like lovers
touching blued skins, giggling
bluish giggles, dreaming
of Bluey bears and nymphs and the hearts
of mandarins where orange is black
like an orange in blue light.

Melody and Caprice

The log pranged him into parts
& pinned him &

He thought, "you think
the weirdest things
at the weirdest times." He thought,
as he watched the blood choir blue to new red
from his wrist
where the bone blade broke through, he thought,
"I want to resurrect Song
and make it the
quiet particle of my Jewel.
I want to joist the baroque and cryptic lung.
I want to jig in the spasm of living
like a fibrillar heart
or a long desperate gasp from a drowning man."

Cedar spice
filled his nostril and his chest.
He sucked it in like opium.

"That. There. That
silvery Lamé of Breath
That Ducasse urge;
that little evil push; the rivulet
of Melody and Caprice; the quintescent
purple goad.

I want watery Song;
green and blue and black
and dangerous and sinuous and lovely as a man's hands."

He thought he thought this.
But he thought, also, he wasn't sure.
"Life is oozy" he giggled into the bark
before he felt the piss trickle down his trousers
as he passed out.

I say

I say "milky way" when we kiss.
I say "your last was a fool"
        when we sleep on
        each other's sweat.
I say "air, air, I need air" when you lead me
        out of the floor
        with your tongue.
I say "I'm afraid of the dark"
        when you stay the guttural
        weekend at your sister's.
I lisp naught things when
        counting tea leaves in
        an auburn bistro
        somewhere uptown.
I say "perfume eh" when we clench
        under migrant harlequin
        shadows in Stanley Park.
I say "pretence, pretence, pretence"
        when we visit
        Seattle and the gaggle
        of second cousins and aunts there.
I say "tulips, orchids and hearts"
        when we sip handfuls
        of painted water from some long
        lost medieval pond; virgin
        glass bubbling mad
        with sour visions of Ophelia
        in our guilty palms.
I say "shrapnel salad" when
        you gurgle and rage about
        Sally, Linda and Therese
        (I also say "I'm sorry").

I blabber "hibernation is a great way to die"
        to myself in the crusty guts
        of an acrylic tube, spitting
        up oxygen and carbon
        all the while.
I say "toast'n'jam huh?"
        as I smear
        celluloid ovaries all about
        my black breakfast (I also
        say "my lungs are broke; baby
        come back" I say that).
I say "staples make funny earrings"
        to the mirror and the wicked
        trafficked man within
        blinking away the bloody thorns.
I say "love is a scampering moss"
        to the flies, and I say
        "watch that it doesn't grab your feet
        and turn you to mould"
        they are flies and don't understand.
I say "clap, and rack 'em up"
        to the pigeon-assed
        stripper downtown, as I
        stroke the cue
        and break my balls again.
I say "that's a buck"
        to the dandruff flake on his shoulder
        (I'm getting good at this game).
I scream "rain, blast you, rain"
        to the abortion sky.
        It rains
        and I slash my wrists with feathers
        and soap and shower in Time's plasma.

I say "paper money, paper laughter"
        to the Modigliani whores
        who clamber for shore when
        Vancouver's streets become
        bloated tributaries.
I say "June, maybe August"
        to the heat that licks
        about me
        in a psychopathic scabbard.
I say "I am a soldier" to the ice
        that melts like your
        groin on my corn
        syrup skin.
I say "here I come Vincent,
        you spastic magician" laying
        the razor to scraps
        of my gift-wrapped
        body for my own wayward prostitute.
I say "blessed be the night"
        when the razor turns to
        postmarks from virgin waters
        and harlequin parks,
        slashing, all the same,
        my littered eyes.
I say "glitter is for diamonds and
        the faceted eyes of bees"
        at your
        slattered photograph
        crusading my piano.
I say "some sort of galaxy"
        when we concile over
        a sacrificial rack of lamb.

I say your last is a fool
        when I sleep
        like a sponge
        on your cool, casual sweat.
I mouth "forever"
        in sympathy with bedsheets,
        whales, and teacups;
        and all fragile things
        pinioned under slabs
        by moist-crashing bodies.
and I whisper "oblivion" and other drugs,
        as I shoot up all of you
        in a quivering; fixed
upon your mute ecstasy.

Man Muttered Motto

Forward.
Plush forward. Plush
indolent forward.
Not so much forward as onward.
Not so much onward as on.
Plush on. Plush
indolent on.
There.
That's it.

On, more decay-like than hydraulic.
Vectorless and Brooding.
Soft and inevitable as love. Rude
like love. Evil
like love. Painful
as ecstasy. Perfumed like Pain.

Rolling. No. Not
rolling. Rubbing. Thawing
and Eroding. Subtractive. Rubbing
like thighs and arms and groins. Rubbing
like stone and moraine and the dull glacial
cunt. Rubbing
like poem-stuff.
Rubbing and rounding pages and manners.
Plush like rolled stones
and salmon roe
and Life-smush.

Adjunct to Marie

Tell your mother
there are small accessories
to the Thing of living; little
ginger stoats that
ripple inside the purple
holes of your muddy
labyrinth; that Chemist
the chlorophyll of your straw;
that Druid your violet fluids.

Tell your mother, then,
the salt that hides
in your skin and groin and blood
is food for
the spawn of Pelicans
and is sowed into
the Carthage of your belly
and turned to taffy
by the engine of your stride.

The Dreams of Pasiphae

There is a revenge to flesh,
a haunt of pulse, a bowel's
lurch, phantom idols
in the folds of the cunt
& a harumph
in the pulp of her tongue.

The gods give spasms
to wifey thighs & manifest
the seed of bulls in dreams
to soot the wombs of queens.
This joining brings
a queer sleep full of
pelvic iron, bruised shoulders
& an issue of nightmares
with mazed placentae.

Recent titles from Turnstone Press

Jerusalem, beloved
   poetry by Di Brandt

Animate Objects
   poetry by Alan Wilson

Body, Inc.: A Theory of Translation Poetics
   criticism by Pamela Banting

Catch as Catch
   poetry by Robert Budde

Lunar Wake
   poetry by Catherine Hunter

Dorothy Livesay's Poetics of Desire
   criticism by Nadine McInnis

Blasphemer's Wheel
   selected and new poetry by Patrick Friesen

Girl by the Water
   poetry by Gary Geddes